BE
BRAVE

Published by Familius LLC, www.familius.com

Familius books are available at special discounts for bulk purchases, whether for sales promotions or for family or corporate use. For more information, contact Familius Sales at 559-876-2170 or email orders@familius.com. Reproduction of this book in any manner, in whole or in part, without written permission of the publisher is prohibited.

Library of Congress Cataloging-in-Publication Data
2017937594

Print ISBN 9781945547263
Ebook ISBN 9781945547560
Printed in China
Edited by Sarah Echard
Illustrated and designed by Adam Eastburn
Cover design by David Miles

10 9 8 7 6 5 4 3 2 1 First Edition

BE
BRAVE

Compiled by Trish Madson

Illustrations by Adam Eastburn

A brave man acknowledges the strength of others.

VERONICA ROTH, *DIVERGENT*

Don't be afraid of your
fears. They're not there
to scare you. They're
there to let you know that
something is worth it.

C. JOYBELL C.

You can, you should,
and if you're brave
enough to start,
you will.

STEPHEN KING, *ON WRITING*

Expose yourself to your deepest fear. After that, fear has no power, and the fear of freedom shrinks and vanishes. You are free.

JIM MORRISON

Scared is what
you're feeling...
but brave is what
you're doing.

EMMA DONOGHUE, *ROOM*

It's not the size of the dog in the fight; it's the size of the fight in the dog.

Courage

is found in unlikely places.

J. R. R. TOLKIEN,
THE FELLOWSHIP OF THE RING

Be brave enough to start a
conversation that matters.

ANONYMOUS

The moment we begin to fear the opinions of others and hesitate to tell the truth that is in us and from motives of policy are silent when we should speak, the divine floods of light and life no longer flow into our souls.

ELIZABETH CADY STANTON

Freedom lies
in being bold.

ROBERT FROST

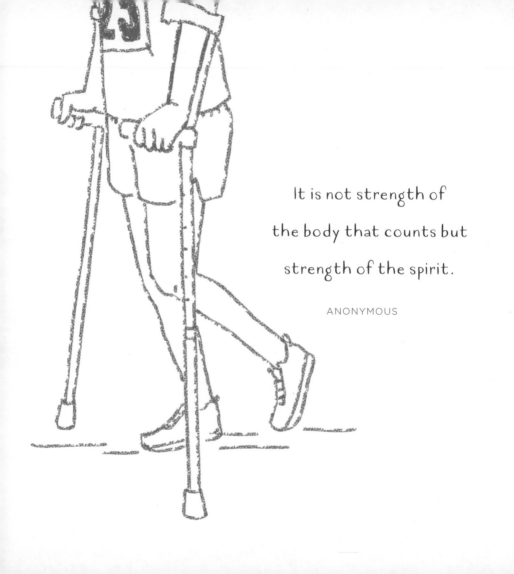

It is not strength of
the body that counts but
strength of the spirit.

ANONYMOUS

When times are hard, summon the
courage to just take the next step.

ANONYMOUS

We cannot be sure of having something to live for unless we are willing to die for it.

CHE GUEVARA

I believe that the most important
single thing, beyond discipline and
creativity, is daring to dare.

MAYA ANGELOU

You can't be brave if you've only had wonderful things happen to you.

MARY TYLER MOORE

A coward is incapable of
exhibiting love; it is the
prerogative of the brave.

MAHATMA GANDHI

One has to understand that
braveness is not the absence of fear
but rather the strength to keep on
going forward despite the fear.

PAULO COELHO

Bravery hides

in amazing places.

KIERA CASS, *THE ONE*

Staying silent is like a slow-growing cancer to the soul and a trait of a true coward. There is nothing intelligent about not standing up for yourself. You may not win every battle. However, everyone will at least know what you stood for —YOU.

SHANNON L. ALDER

It is hard to be brave ... when you're
only a Very Small Animal.

A. A. MILNE, *WINNIE THE POOH*

The bravest thing I ever did was
continuing my life when
I wanted to die.

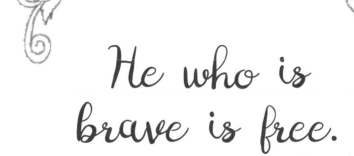

He who is
brave is free.

SENECA

Courage and perseverance have
a magical talisman, before
which difficulties disappear and
obstacles vanish into air.

JOHN QUINCY ADAMS

When a brave man takes a
stand, the spines of others
are often stiffened.

BILLY GRAHAM

Courage is the price that life exacts

for granting peace.

AMELIA EARHART

The future doesn't belong to the fainthearted. It belongs to the brave.

RONALD REAGAN

I want to be someone strong and
brave enough to make hard choices.
But I want to be fair and loving
enough to make the right ones.

AMY ENGEL, *THE BOOK OF IVY*

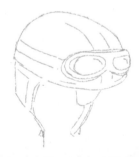

Difficulties mastered are

opportunities won.

WINSTON CHURCHILL

We must constantly build
dikes of courage to hold
back the flood of fear.

MARTIN LUTHER KING JR.

Nobody can hurt me
without my permission.

MAHATMA GANDHI

You'll never be brave if you don't get hurt.

You'll never learn if you don't make mistakes.

You'll never be a success if you don't encounter failure.

ANONYMOUS

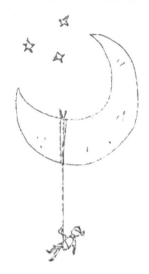

Bravery comes one
day at a time.

COURTNEY C. STEVENS,
FAKING NORMAL

There is a great difference between
being fearless and being brave.

PATRICK ROTHFUSS,
THE NAME OF THE WIND

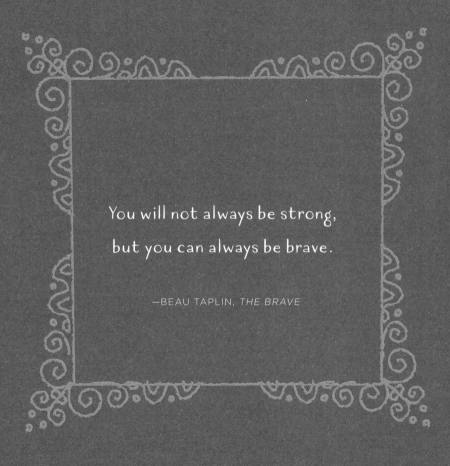

You will not always be strong,

but you can always be brave.

—BEAU TAPLIN, *THE BRAVE*

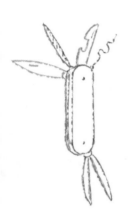

Smiling at death seems like a
pretty bold act. And so I smile
like a damned fool.

EMM COLE, *KEEPING MERMINIA*

Always have faith in yourself and
the universe, for one will not get
you anywhere without the other.
Both must be equally strong
to reach your desires, for they are
the wings that will lift you
to your dreams.

SUZY KASSEM,
RISE UP AND SALUTE THE SUN

Be brave

enough to live the life of your

dreams according to

your vision and purpose

instead of the expectations and

opinions of others.

ROY BENNETT,

THE LIGHT IN THE HEART

Those who can truly be accounted
brave are those who best know the
meaning of what is sweet in
life and what is terrible, and
then go out, undeterred, to meet
what is to come.

PERICLES

To embark on the journey towards your goals and dreams requires bravery. To remain on that path requires courage. The bridge that merges the two is commitment.

STEVE MARABOLI,
UNAPOLOGETICALLY YOU

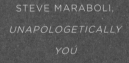

The brave man carves out his fortune, and every man is the sum of his own works.

MIGUEL DE CERVANTES

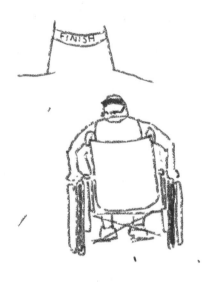

I find my greatest strength in wanting to be strong. I find my greatest bravery in deciding to be brave...If there's no feeling of fear, then there's no need for courage.

DAVID LEVITHAN, *BOY MEETS BOY*

Courage in the path is what makes
the path manifest itself.

PAULO COELHO

All brave men love; for he only is brave who has affections to fight for, whether in the daily battle of life, or in physical contests.

WILLIAM COWPER PRIME,

THE OLD HOUSE BY THE RIVER

To go against the grain
Is the secret to bravey.

DEJAN STOJANOVIC,

"SIMPLICITY"

We never know how high we are
Till we are called to rise;
And then, if we are true to plan,
Our statures touch the skies.

EMILY DICKINSON,
"WE NEVER KNOW HOW HIGH WE ARE"

Bravado may stir the crowd, but

courage needs no audience.

T. F. HODGE,

FROM WITHIN I RISE

Bravery is a willing decision to do what must be done. Fear is a cancer that is cured only by doing what must be done, backed by an intellgent, open mind.

COREY AARON BÛRKES

I'm done waiting for someone...
to save me. Today I'll be the
one doing the saving.

PAM BACHORZ, *DROUGHT*

History, despite wrenching pain,

Cannot be unlived, but if faced

With courage, need not be lived again.

MAYA ANGELOU,
"ON THE PULSE OF MORNING"

Bravery is when you walk into a battle you are not sure of winning.

JEFFREY FRY

What makes us brave isn't lacking
the good sense to be afraid;
it's looking back at what we've
lived through and seeing
if we faced it well.

CAITLIN R. KIERNAN

Survival, my only hope.

Success, my only revenge.

Sarcasm, my only weapon.

Bravery, my only shield.

FARIA REHMAN

Every person has the power to change their fate if they are brave enough to fight for what they desire more than anything.

Fear echoes your self-defined limitations, not your actual ones. To change your self-image, you must face what scares you.

VIRONIKA TUGALEVA

Problems don't get better with time; they become better when you find bravery. Success demands that you fight your fears.

ADAM KIRK SMITH

The courage to live brings its own rewards.

RACHEL L. SCHADE,

THE SILENT KINGDOM

Stand up and let the world hear
your roar; now spread your wings
and begin to soar.

MYA WAECHTLER

He was mad
and plenty
brave.

ERNEST HEMMINGWAY,

TO HAVE AND HAVE NOT

Sometimes it isn't fighting that's
brave; it's facing the death
you know is coming.

VERONICA ROTH, *DIVERGENT*

Those of you who are brave enough
to venture out find so many things
that we never knew within.

LINDA POINDEXTER

If you're brave enough to get
through the darkness then you
shall shine in the light.

MATTHEW DONNELLY

Where you are and what you have
been through has you perfectly
placed to move forward.
Stronger, braver, wiser.

TONY CURL

If you're brave enough to say
goodbye, life will reward
you with a new hello.

PAULO COELHO

They outnumbered me, and I was
worsted and under their feet; but,
as yet, I was not dead.

CHARLOTTE BRONTË, *VILLETTE*

Courage cannot be unveiled without reality.

MUNIA KHAN

You may not control all the events
that happen to you, but you can
decide not to be reduced by them.

MAYA ANGELOU,
LETTER TO MY DAUGHTER

A river cuts through a rock
not because of its power
but its persistence.

ANONYMOUS

It is good to be brave;

it is better to be good;

strive to be both.

JUSTIN MCCARTHY

Reality is a dream that someone was brave enough to conquer.

SHANNON L. ALDER

If I rise up again against the foe,

dare I stand alone?

T. A. CLINE, *ARCHOMAI*

To be brave is to behave
Bravely when your heart is faint.
So you can be really brave
Only when you really ain't.

PIET HEIN

Empaths did not come into
this world to be victims;
we came to be warriors.
Be brave. Stay strong.
We need all hands on deck.

ANTHON ST. MAARTEN

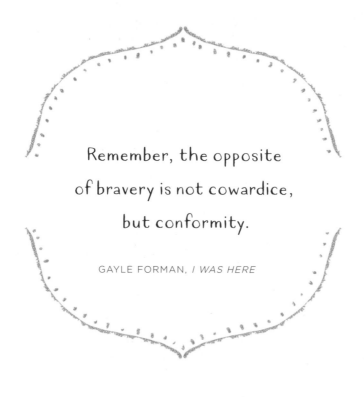

Remember, the opposite
of bravery is not cowardice,
but conformity.

GAYLE FORMAN, *I WAS HERE*

Isn't bravery always sort of beautiful?

STEPHEN KING, *LISEY'S STORY*

Rise up oh heart,
for there is another
battle to win.

T. A. CLINE

And then eventually you wake up, fully rested, ready to fly again.

CASS VAN KRAH

Sometimes one act of bravery is better than a life lived as a coward.

AMITA TRASI,
THE COLOR OF OUR SKY

If you're waiting until you feel
talented enough to make it,
you'll never make it.

CRISS JAMI, *HEALOLOGY*

How can you follow your heart,
unless you know why you have
allowed it to be empty for
so long and didn't have the
courage to fix it?

SHANNON L. ALDER

I know of no better or quicker way
to step into my greatness than to
step out of what's familiar.

VIRONIKA TUGALEVA

When you have nothing to hide,

you have nothing to fear.

ANONYMOUS

I can't be my own person if I constantly require someone else to hold me together.

TAHEREH MAFI

Virtue is bold, and goodness never fearful.

It is far easier to see brave men die
than to hear a coward beg for life.

JACK LONDON, *THE IRON HEEL*

Courage injures the strong ones
who have no wisdom, but it
motivates the brave
ones to always win.

AULIQ ICE

Courage is rightly esteemed
the first of human qualities ...
because it is the quality which
guarantees all others.

WINSTON CHURCHILL

Bravery is a lot less formal than it sounds. Bravery is being able to have a conversation with a stranger. It's going back to school even after years of being away. It's being you even when it's easier to be someone else.

MARQUITE BURKE-DEJESUS

O, that's a brave man!

He writes brave verses,

Speaks brave words,

swears brave oaths and breaks

Them bravely.

WILLIAM SHAKESPEARE,

AS YOU LIKE IT

Be at your best when things

are at their worst.

ANONYMOUS

Kites rise highest against the wind
—not with it.

WINSTON CHURCHILL

It takes a strong person to stand up to his or her fate and overcome the obstacles that stand in the way of freedom and success, but I believe in you.

PAX PRENTISS,

THE ALCOHOLISM AND ADDICTION CURE

It is the bravery of the lion that enables you the lion's share of the power. More important than all, know this: bravery begets victory.

S. A. BOURALEH,
THE SERPENT'S SON

I think the bravest people are not
the ones brave enough to die but
the ones brave enough to live. And
living is different than surviving.

AUDREY CELIA

"The coward dies a thousand deaths,

the brave but one?"

"Of course. Who said it?"

"I don't know."

"He was probably a coward," she said. "He

knew a great deal about cowards but nothing

about the brave. The brave dies perhaps two

thousand deaths if he's intelligent. He simply

doesn't mention them.

ERNEST HEMMINGWAY,

A FAREWELL TO ARMS

I have the heart of a man,
not a woman, and I am not
afraid of anything.

ELIZABETH I

I beg you take courage; the brave
soul can mend even disaster.

CATHERINE THE GREAT

Acts of love, for me,

are leaps of bravery.

ANNA WHITE, *MENDED*

Do the little things. In the future when you look back, they'd have made the greatest change.

NIKE THADDEUS

Be bold enough to use your voice,
brave enough to listen to your
heart, and strong enough to live
the life you've always imagined.

ANONYMOUS

Fearing our confrontations is one thing...facing them unarmed is a completely different matter.

MARK W. BOYER

Your personal declaration of will is the first step in a seemingly impossible journey.

BRYANT MCGILL, *VOICE OF REASON*

Dare to be brave today,
and trust that when you extend
your wings, you will fly.

MARY E. DEMUTH, *EVERYTHING*

It takes bravery to recognize
where in your life you are
your own poison . . .
it takes courage to
do something about it.

STEVE MARABOLI,

UNAPOLOGETICALLY YOU

A brave action is often followed by grief. Do not let my resistance to grief stop the brave action.

ALANIS MORISSETTE

Bravery is measured by how hard
you try, not by whether you
actually succeed.

NANCY STRAIGHT, *BLOOD DEBT*

Brave men don't belong to
any one country. I respect bravery
wherever I see it.

HARRY TRUMAN

If it must be
done, it's best
done bravely.

COURTNEY MILAN, *UNLOCKED*

Many have stood their ground and faced the darkness when it comes for them. Fewer come for the darkness and force it to face them.

ELIEZER YUDOWSKY,

HARRY POTTER AND THE METHODS OF RATIONALITY

We could never learn to be
brave and patient if there were
only joy in the world.

HELEN KELLER

Forgiveness is a virtue of the brave.

INDIRA GANDHI

The real man smiles in trouble,
gathers strength from distress, and
grows brave by reflection.

THOMAS PAINE

Courage is being scared to death but saddling up anyways.

JOHN WAYNE

Be brave—even if you're not,
pretend to be. No one will
know the difference.

ANONYMOUS

One doesn't discover new lands
without consenting to lose sight,
for a very long time, of the shore.

ANDRÉ GIDE, *LES FAUX-MONNAYEURS*

If it scares you, it might
be a good thing to try.

SETH GODIN

You never know how strong
you are until being strong is the only
option you have left.

ANONYMOUS

We shall draw from the heart
of suffering itself the means of
inspiration and survival.

WINSTON CHURCHILL

The courage of life is often a less dramatic spectacle than the courage of a final moment; but it is no less a magnificent mixture of triumph and tragedy.

JOHN F. KENNEDY,
PROFILES IN COURAGE

Stop being afraid of what could go wrong and start being positive about what could go right.

ANONYMOUS

I learned that courage was not the absence of fear, but the triumph over it. The brave man is not he who does not feel afraid but he who conquers that fear.

NELSON MANDELA,
LONG WALK TO FREEDOM

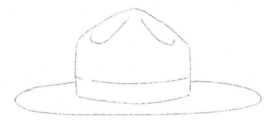

Look to the past with wisdom, and

look to the future with courage.

STACEY T. HUNT

You are confined only by the

walls you build yourself.

ANONYMOUS

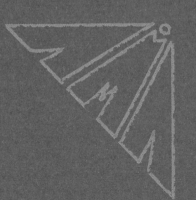
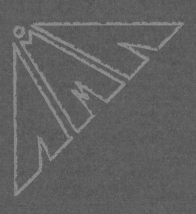

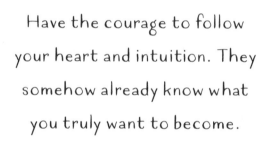

Have the courage to follow
your heart and intuition. They
somehow already know what
you truly want to become.

STEVE JOBS

You are braver than you believe,
stronger than you seem, and
smarter than you think.

POOH'S GRAND ADVENTURE: THE

SEARCH FOR CHRISTOPHER ROBIN, 1997

Experimentation is the
precursor to wisdom. Be bold.
Be brave. Make mistakes.
Truth follows the courageous.

Only those who will risk going
too far can possibly find out
how far one can go.

T. S. ELIOT, AS WRITTEN IN THE PREFACE TO

TRANSIT OF VENUS BY HARRY CROSBY

It takes courage to grow up and

become who you really are.

E. E. CUMMINGS

Courage is a love affair

with the unknown.

OSHO

People are made of flesh and blood
and a miracle fibre called courage.

MIGNON MCLAUGHLIN,
THE NEUROTIC'S NOTEBOOK

Sometimes even to live is

an act of courage.

SENECA,

MORAL LETTERS TO LUCILIUS

Courage can't see around corners,

but goes around them anyway.

MIGNON MCLAUGHLIN,

THE NEUROTIC'S NOTBOOK

Courage is the power to let
go of the familiar.

RAYMOND LINDQUIST

Courage is as often the outcome
of despair as of hope; in the one
case we have nothing to lose, in the
other everything to gain.

DIANE DE POITIERS

Courage is to feel the daily
daggers of relentless steel
and keep on living.

DOUGLAS MALLOCH

Courage ought to have
eyes as well as arms.

H. G. BOCH

We may encounter many defeats,
but we must not be defeated.

MAYA ANGELOU

Kind heart,
fierce mind,
brave spirit.

ANONYMOUS

To believe yourself brave is to be brave; it is the one only essential thing.

MARK TWAIN, *JOAN OF ARC*

Be brave enough to live life
creatively. The creative is the place
where no one else has ever been.

ALAN ALDA

Perhaps all the dragons of our lives
are princesses who are only waiting
to see us once beautiful and brave.

RAINIER MARIA RILKE,

"LETTERS TO A YOUNG POET"

I'm not funny. What I am is brave.

LUCILLE BALL ·

Live as brave men; and if fortune
is adverse, front its blows
with brave hearts.

CICERO

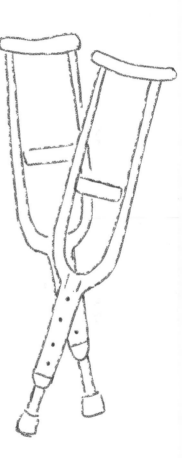

Sometimes the hardest

battle is with yourself.

ANONYMOUS

Neither a wise man nor a brave man lies down on the tracks of history to wait for the train of the future to run over him.

DWIGHT D. EISENHOWER

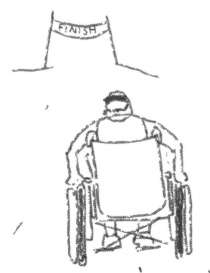

The pressure of adversity does
not affect the mind of the brave
men...It is more powerful than
external circumstances.

SENECA

In the flush of love's light

We dare be brave

And suddenly we see

That love costs all we are

And will ever be

Yet it is only love

Which sets us free.

MAYA ANGELOU,

"TOUCHED BY AN ANGEL"

Physical courage, which despises all
danger, will make a man brave
in one way and moral courage,
which despises all opinion, will make
a man brave in another.

THE RAILROAD TRAINMAN,

VOLUME 12

No one is so brave that
he is not disturbed by
something unexpected.

JULIUS CAESAR

It is vain for the coward to flee;

death follows close behind;

it is only by defying it that

the brave escape.

VOLTAIRE

Conscience in the soul is the
root of all true courage; if a
man would be brave, let him
learn to obey his conscience.

JAMES FREEMAN CLARKE

We become just by doing just acts,
temperate by doing temperate acts,
brave by doing brave acts.

ARISTOTLE, *NICOMACHEAN ETHICS*

People are capable, at any time in their lives, of doing what they dream of.

A brave man is a man who dares to look the devil in the face and tell him he is a devil.

JAMES A. GARFIELD

The wise never doubt.
The humane never worry.
The brave never fear.

CONFUCIUS, *THE ANALECTS*

Strength does not come from
physical capacity. It comes
from an indomitable will.

MAHATMA GANDHI

One man with courage

makes a majority.

ANONYMOUS

The law of sacrifice is uniform
throughout the world.
To be effective, it demands the
sacrifice of the bravest and
the most spotless.

MAHATMA GANDHI

The ultimate measure of a man is
not where he stands in moments
of comfort and convenience,
but where he stands at times of
challenge and controversy.

MARTIN LUTHER KING JR.

He is as full of valour as of kindness;

Princely in both.

WILLIAM SHAKESPEARE,

HENRY V

No one saves us but ourselves.

No one can and no one may.

We ourselves must walk the path.

ANONYMOUS

You yourself, as much as anybody
in the entire universe, deserve
your love and affection.

SHARON SALZBERG

Never give in, never give in,

never, never, never, never.

WINSTON CHURCHILL

Courage is what it takes to stand
up and speak; courage is also what it
takes to sit down and listen.

ANONYMOUS

Being brave means that
knowing when you fail,
you won't fail forever.

LANA DEL REY

This is no time for ease and comfort. It is time to dare and endure.

WINSTON CHURCHILL

Some have been thought brave

because they were afraid

to run away.

THOMAS FULLER

Sometimes all you need is twenty
seconds of insane courage...
And I promise you, something
great will come of it.

WE BOUGHT A ZOO, 2011

It's not bravery to walk through
the jungle with a lion's escort,
but it is with a rabbit.

FAZLI RREZJA

A wise woman wishes to be no one's enemy; a wise woman refuses to be anyone's victim.

MAYA ANGELOU

I believe that courage
is the sum of strength and
wisdom. You take away wisdom
from the equation—courage
may turn to rage.

DODINSKY

Sometimes the bravest thing you
can do is let someone love you.

N. R. HART, *POETRY AND PEARLS*

We are liberated by the examples
of the brave, the talented,
and the successful if we allow
ourselves that freedom.

TERESA COLLINS,
LIVE LIFE IN ALL CAPS

Courage is reckoned the greatest
of all virtues; because, unless a man
has that virtue, he has no security
for preserving any other.

SAMUEL JOHNSON

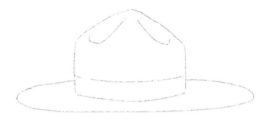

Once we believe in ourselves, we can
risk curiosity, wonder, spontaneous
delight, or any experience that
reveals the human spirit.

E. E. CUMMINGS

The best way out is always through.

ROBERT FROST,

"A SERVANT TO SERVANTS"

Don't consider my kindness as weakness. The beast inside is sleeping, not dead.

ANONYMOUS

Being brave enough to just
be unapologetic for who
you are; that's a goddess.

BANKS

It is curious that physical courage
should be so common in the world and
moral courage so rare.

MARK TWAIN

Turn your wounds into wisdom.

ANONYMOUS

If there is no struggle,

there is no progress.

FREDERICK DOUGLASS

Breathe. Let go. And remind
yourself that this very moment
is the only one you know
you have for sure.

OPRAH WINFREY

Be sure and put your feet in the right place, and then stand firm.

ABRAHAM LINCOLN

All our dreams can come true,
if we have the courage
to pursue them.

WALT DISNEY

You don't develop courage by being happy every day. You develop it by surviving difficult times and challenging adversity.

BARBARA DE ANGELIS

You gain strength, courage,
and confidence by every experience
in which you really stop to look
fear in the face. You are able to say
to yourself, "I lived through this
horror. I can take the next
thing that comes along."

ELEANOR ROOSEVELT

We draw our strength from the very despair in which we have been forced to live. We shall endure.

CESAR CHAVEZ

Be strong when you are weak.

Be brave when you are scared.

Be humble when you are victorious.

ANONYMOUS

Our fate lives within us; you only
have to be brave enough to see it.

BRAVE, 2012

Bravery is believing in yourself, and that thing nobody can teach you.

EL CORDOBÉS

She is clothed in strength and
dignity, and she laughs without
fear of the future.

PROVERBS 31:25 NLT

Good women play by the rules.

Brave women make the rules.

Be strong enough to stand
alone, smart enough to know
when you need help, and brave
enough to ask for it.

ZIAD K. ABDELNOUR

Bravery is looking into
[someone's] eyes without
shivering and compromising.

M. F. MOONZAJER

The struggle you're in today is
developing the strength you
need for tomorrow.

ROBERT TEW

Many of the bravest never are
known, and get no praise. [But]
that does not lessen their beauty.

LOUISA MAY ALCOTT,
EIGHT COUSINS

You cannot change the world by
being like the world. Stand alone.
Stand apart. Stand out. Stand for
something. Stand up and be brave.

ANONYMOUS

Holding on is being brave,
but letting go and moving on
is often what makes us
stronger and happier.

MARC CHERNOFF

You must never be fearful about
what you're doing when it is right.

ROSA PARKS

When the whole world is silent,

even one voice becomes powerful.

MALALA YOUSAFZAI

Take chances; make mistakes.
That's how you grow. Pain nourishes
your courage. You have to fail in
order to practice being brave.

MARY TYLER MOORE

Life shrinks or expands in

proportion with one's courage.

ANAÏS NIN

About the Author

Trish Madson is a lifelong book enthusiast with over twenty years experience in the publishing and entertainment industry. Her true passion is creating books that inspire and encourage children to learn while ultimately having fun. When she's not working on children's books, she enjoys reading, taking advantage of the amazing year-round outdoor activities in the Pacific Northwest, spending time with her family, and hanging out on the beach. You can find a complete history of Trish's work experience on LinkedIn.

About the Illustrator

Adam Eastburn is an up-and-coming artist from California. By day, he is a graphic and motion designer; by night, an illustrator and animator. Adam and his wife, Denise, enjoy travel and James Bond flicks. Find more of his work at adameastburn.net.